THE GREAT OUTDOORS

FRESHWATER FISHING

Revised and Updated

by Ellen Hopkins

Consultant:
John Dettloff
National Fresh Water Fishing Hall of Fame
Hayward, Wisconsin

Capstone
press
Mankato, Minnesota

Edge Books are published by Capstone Press,
151 Good Counsel Drive, P.O. Box 669, Mankato, Minnesota 56002.
www.capstonepress.com

Library of Congress Cataloging-in-Publication Data
Hopkins, Ellen.
Freshwater fishing / by Ellen Hopkins.—Rev. and updated.
p. cm.—(Edge books. Great outdoors)
Includes bibliographical references and index.
ISBN-13: 978-1-4296-0820-6 (hardcover)
ISBN-10: 1-4296-0820-X (hardcover)
1. Fishing—Juvenile literature. I. Title. II. Series.
SH445.H67 2008
799.1'1—dc22   2007012281

Summary: Describes the equipment, skills, conservation issues, and safety concerns of
freshwater fishing.

Editorial Credits
Carrie Braulick, editor; Katy Kudela, photo researcher; Jenny Krueger, revised edition
editor; Thomas Emery, revised edition designer; Kyle Grenz, revised edition
production designer

Photo Credits
Capstone Press/Gary Sundermeyer, 5, 9, 13, 15, 16, 19, 20, 22, 25, 28, 30–31, 39;
Karon Dubke, cover
Jeff Henry/Roche Jaune Pictures, Inc., 7, 41
Photo Network/Jim Schwabel, 36
Photri-Microstock, 42
Rob and Ann Simpson, 44
Unicorn Stock Photos/Aneal Vohra, 34
Visuals Unlimited/Patrice Ceisel, 43; Steve Maslowski, 45
Wikipedia, public-domain image, 10–11
William H. Mullins, 33

1 2 3 4 5 6 12 11 10 09 08 07

TABLE OF CONTENTS

Essential content terms are highlighted and are defined at the bottom of the page where they first appear.

Chapter 1

FRESHWATER FISHING

Learn about the history of freshwater fishing and types of freshwater fish.

People have been freshwater fishing for thousands of years. It is one of North America's most popular sports. There are many freshwater streams, rivers, and lakes in North America for people to fish.

History of Fishing

Prehistoric people hunted animals and gathered plants to survive. Historians believe that the most successful early people also fished. These people used pieces of bone, wood, or stone called gorges. The gorges were about 1 inch (2.5 centimeters) long. They were pointed at both ends. People covered the gorges with bait and attached a line to them. The gorge would stick in a fish's throat after the fish swallowed the bait.

Anglers can freshwater fish from a dock, lakeshore, or boat.

Egyptian artwork from 2000 B.C. shows people fishing with rods, lines, and nets. Ancient Greek and Roman writings also have accounts of people fishing.

Fish were a major source of food for American Indians. They often used spears to pierce fish. This type of fishing is called spearfishing. Many American Indians still practice this today.

In the early 1700s, people began to use rods with reels to fish. The reels were made of wooden spools. They allowed people to fish farther away from shore. People used the reels to quickly bring in or let out long lengths of line.

Today, most people fish with modern rods and reels. The sport is also called angling. Many North Americans angle both for recreation and for a source of food.

EDGE FACT

A traditional form of fishing still used today is to fish with cane poles made from bamboo or cut from small, young trees.

Anglers fish in freshwater sources such as streams, rivers, ponds, and lakes.

Types of Freshwater Fish

Anglers try to catch various types of freshwater fish. These fish live in water that contains very little or no salt. Freshwater includes streams, rivers, ponds, and lakes. Saltwater fish live in the world's seas and oceans.

Some anglers try to catch small fish species such as white crappies and bluegill. These small fish are called panfish. Panfish live in shallow water close to shore. Panfish eat insects, minnows, and worms. Minnows are small fish about 2 inches (5 centimeters) long.

Anglers also try to catch large fish such as northern pike and muskellunge, or muskies. These fish hunt small fish, frogs, and sometimes even ducklings. They have sharp, pointed teeth. They live in deep areas of lakes near plants.

North American anglers also try to catch catfish. Catfish are bottom feeders. They eat small animals and plants at the bottom of a body of water. Catfish species include the bullhead, the flathead, the blue, and the channel.

Many anglers fish for trout and bass. Trout live in cool, fast-running streams. These fish usually eat insects. Bass live in streams, rivers, and lakes.

species—a group of animals with similar features

Battered Fillets

Serves: 4-6   *Children should have adult supervision.*

Ingredients:
1 cup (250 mL) flour
1 cup (250 mL) cornmeal
1 egg
1/2 cup milk (125 mL)
4 small fish fillets (boneless)
About 5 tablespoons (75 mL) oil
Salt and pepper
Lemon wedges

Equipment:
Small bowl
Large plate
Medium bowl
Spoon, egg beater,
  or automatic mixer
Large frying pan
Metal spatula
Paper towels

What You Do:
1. Combine flour and cornmeal in a small bowl and spread the mixture on a large plate.
2. Beat egg in medium bowl with spoon, egg beater, or mixer. Add milk. Continue to beat until combined.
3. Dip each fish fillet in egg and milk mixture.
4. Press both sides of each fillet in flour and cornmeal mixture.
5. Add oil to frying pan until the bottom is covered about 1/4 inch (.6 centimeter) deep. Heat oil over medium-high heat until the oil becomes shiny and hot.
6. Sprinkle salt and pepper over the fillets.
7. Fry fillets about 5 minutes or until coating is golden brown. Turn fillets once with spatula. Repeat on the other side.
8. Drain on paper towels. Serve with lemon wedges.

Giant Catfish!

EDGE FACT ⸻⊙

Most kinds of catfish are not nearly as large as the Mekong giant catfish. The average size of a channel catfish, for example, is between 2 and 4 pounds (.9 to 1.8 kilograms.)

10

Imagine pulling a fish the size of a grizzly bear out of the water. Fishers in Thailand did just that in 2005. What most people consider the world's largest freshwater catch was a Mekong giant catfish weighing in at 646 pounds (293 kilograms). The terrific catfish measured almost 9 feet (2.7 meters) long. Thai fishermen used a net to haul in the giant from the Mekong River.

Mekong giant catfish are rare. Scientists believe they face extinction. Fewer and fewer of these giant freshwater fish are caught each year. Loss of habitat and dams blocking the rivers where they swim makes it difficult for the giant catfish to survive. The World Wildlife Fund and the National Geographic Society are studying the planet's biggest freshwater fish. With the help of their research, people hope to save the Mekong giant catfish from disappearing for good.

Chapter 2

EQUIPMENT

Learn about fishing gear, including different kinds of rods, reels, and line.

Freshwater anglers need several pieces of equipment. They should have a rod, reel, and fishing line. Anglers also need hooks, bait, and lures. Lures are wood, metal, or plastic objects that are attached to hooks. Anglers use lures to attract fish. Small equipment like this can be kept in a tackle box.

Rods

Anglers can choose from a variety of rod types. Most modern rods are made of fiberglass or graphite. These materials are lightweight and strong.

Anglers use different rod lengths. Most freshwater anglers choose rods that are about 5 to 7 feet (1.5 to 2.1 meters) long. Anglers use short rods for short casts. Long rods allow anglers to cast line farther.

Most rods weigh between 2 and 4.5 pounds (.9 and 2 kilograms). Anglers who plan to catch large, heavy fish choose heavy rods. Anglers who plan to catch small fish choose lightweight rods.

The way a certain rod bends is called action. Fast-action rods bend mostly near the tip. Anglers usually put small bait and lures on fast-action rods. Slow-action rods bend closer to the rod's grip. Anglers often put heavy lures on slow-action rods. Beginning anglers often choose medium-action rods. These rods bend in the middle. They are suitable for a variety of bait and lures.

Some anglers who fish for panfish attach line to cane poles. These simple rods often have no reel. They are usually about 4 feet (1.2 meters) long. Cane poles are good for beginning anglers.

EDGE FACT

Cane poles are much longer than standard rods. They can be up to 10 feet (3 meters) long.

Most anglers use rods that are between 5 and 7 feet (1.5 and 2.1 meters) long.

Reels

Reels allow anglers to control the line and the bait or lure attached to it. They also help anglers bring in hooked fish. Two basic types of freshwater reels are bait casting reels and spinning reels. Bait casting reels are heavier than spinning reels and can handle a great deal of weight.

Close-face reels have a cover and a hole where the line comes out.

Close-face reel

Anglers usually use bait casting reels to catch large fish. Spinning reels are light and easy to cast. Anglers usually use these reels to catch small fish.

Spinning reels may be open-face or close-face. Close-face reels have a plastic cover. The front of the cover has a hole where the line comes out. Open-face reels allow anglers to cast greater distances than close-face reels do. The line rubs against the hole on close-face reels and causes a shorter cast. But close-face reels provide anglers with more control over their cast than open-face reels.

Modern reels have either a push button, bar, or movable bail that puts the reel into freespool. Line is able to come off the reel during freespool. Anglers put the reel into freespool to cast. The weight of the bait or lure pulls line off the spool.

Reels also have an anti-reverse device. After a cast, anglers turn the reel handle. This action engages the anti-reverse device and locks the line in place.

Anglers adjust the reel's drag if they hook a fish. A hooked fish often swims, jumps, or dives. The line could break if it stayed tight. And the fish could wrap the line around obstacles if the line is too loose. The drag on the reel should be set so that there is pressure on the line. But it should also allow a hooked fish to pull line off the reel.

drag—a device at the back of the reel that puts pressure on the line

Line

Anglers choose a line's strength based on the weight of the fish they plan to catch. Strength is measured by how many pounds the line can hold before it breaks. For example, 8-pound (3.6-kilogram) test can hold 8 pounds of pressure without breaking.

Most anglers use nylon monofilament line. This line has a single strand. It is strong and flexible. Multifilament line is made of braided threads of strong plastic called polyethylene. Multifilament line is five times stronger than monofilament line of the same thickness. It can hold larger fish than monofilament line.

Leaders, Sinkers, and Bobbers

Many anglers use leaders, which vary greatly in length. One end of the leader is attached to the hook or lure. The other end is hooked to a swivel at the end of the fishing line. This metal connecting piece has two small round holes.

EDGE FACT

Most fish can see in color. This is one reason lures are made in many different shades.

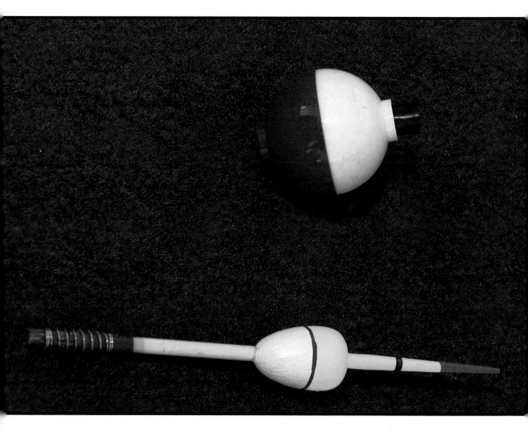

Sinkers are weights that keep bait or lures near the bottom of the water. Anglers may use small balls made of lead or other metals. In some states, anglers are encouraged to avoid using lead sinkers. These sinkers can be harmful to the environment. Sliding sinkers have a hole in the middle. A leader easily slides through these sinkers.

Anglers in boats always should wear life jackets.

Sinkers are sometimes used with bobbers. These small floating objects attach to the line. They keep bait at a certain water depth. Anglers watch the bobber to help them know when a fish takes their bait.

barb—sharp points that extend from behind a fishhook's point

Hooks

Anglers use a variety of fishhooks. Hooks are sized by number. Hooks that have high numbers are smaller than hooks with low numbers. Anglers choose hooks based on the size of fish they want to catch.

Many anglers use barbless hooks. Barbs help the hook stay in a fish's mouth. But barbed hooks are more difficult to remove from a fish's mouth than barbless hooks. Barbless hooks also cause less damage to fish than barbed hooks.

Other Essential Gear

Below are a few other items that fishers should bring on their trip.

- **Clippers**—to cut fishing line
- **Depth Finder**—small electronic devices that display the location of fish on a screen
- **First Aid Kit**
- **Forceps**— to remove a hook from a fish's mouth
- **Hat**—to shade the face from sun
- **Net**—to help handle hooked fish
- **Sunglasses and Sunscreen**

Equipment

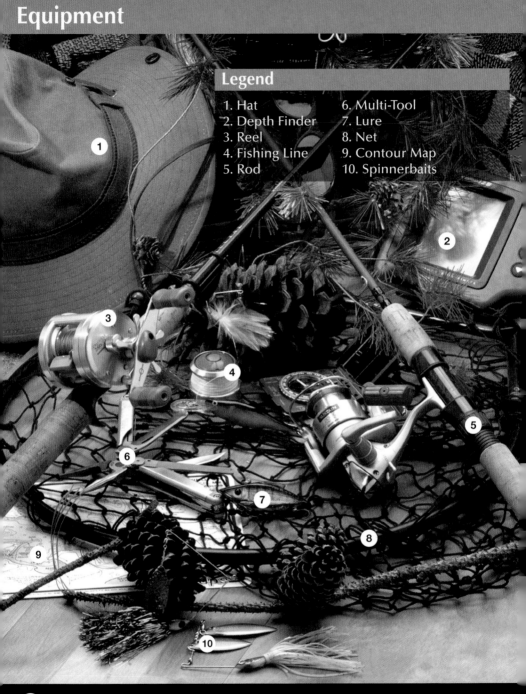

Legend

1. Hat
2. Depth Finder
3. Reel
4. Fishing Line
5. Rod
6. Multi-Tool
7. Lure
8. Net
9. Contour Map
10. Spinnerbaits

The Great Outdoors—Equipment

Some anglers also carry a thermometer to check the water's temperature. The ideal water temperature varies according to the type of fish. For example, panfish and catfish often live in water between 75 and 80 degrees Fahrenheit (24 and 27 degrees Celsius).

Clothing

Anglers should wear clothes that are suitable for the weather. In warm weather, they wear shorts and a short-sleeved shirt. They should also bring warmer clothes in case the weather changes. In colder weather, it is best to dress in layers. Anglers should have a water-resistant jacket in case of rain showers.

Anglers often wear life jackets. Unskilled swimmers and anglers who fish from boats must wear life jackets. Some anglers wear life jackets near streams and rivers with strong currents.

EDGE FACT

Mosquitoes and mayflies are most active around sundown, and they bite! During summer, anglers should wear clothing that leaves little skin exposed.

Chapter 3

SKILLS AND TECHNIQUES

Learn about casting techniques, bait, and lures.

Beginning anglers should know the behaviors of different types of freshwater fish. It is important to learn what bait and lures will attract certain kinds of fish.

Finding Fish

Anglers can look for fish in a number of areas. Fish often lie near objects in the water, including rocks, docks, or submerged trees. Structures offer shady places for fish to hide. Objects can also create areas of slow-moving water called pocket water. Fish rest in pocket water. Fish also gather near edges. Edges may form where fast-moving water meets calm water. They also may form where shallow water meets deep water. The lip of a dam or a line of weeds can form an edge. Edges often hold insects and plankton that fish eat.

edge—a visible line where water changes or plants grow

plankton—tiny plants and animals

Casting

Anglers start a cast with the rod in front of them. Anglers hold the rod in one hand with their palm facing down. They look where they want to cast. They also look around to make sure it is safe to cast.

Several steps make a successful cast. The first step is bending the wrist back to bring the rod behind the shoulder. Fishers wait for the bait or lure to settle. They also make sure the line is not tangled.

The line can then be put into freespool. Anglers who use bait casting reels place their thumb on the line to keep it from unreeling. Anglers who use spinning reels press a button on the reel's bottom. Fishers should continue to look at the target as they quickly move the rod forward. They then lift their index finger or release the button as the leader flies past the rod's tip. This action lets the line out.

Anglers can use a clock face to help them learn how to cast. They first bring the rod behind their shoulder and stop at 10 o' clock. They then start to bring their arm forward. Anglers release the button or lift their finger from the line at 1 o'clock. They stop the cast at 2 o'clock.

Bait and Lures

Anglers present bait where fish would normally find it. For example, anglers place grasshoppers near the water's surface. They place worms near the bottom.

Lures imitate the vibration, color, scent, or movement of food that a fish would eat. Spoons are made of shiny metal. These lures imitate small fish.

You can buy nightcrawlers from a bait shop, or take them from your own backyard!

Minnows

Mealworms

Nightcrawlers

Spinners have a thin blade that turns as anglers pull it through the water. Spinnerbaits and buzzbaits vibrate and shine.

Plugs imitate small fish, frogs, or mice. Some plugs float. Others sink to attract bottom feeders. Some plugs are crankbaits. Anglers reel in these lures underwater to attract fish.

Anglers may also use surface plugs. These lures float on the water's surface. Surface plugs are sometimes called topwaters.

Some anglers use jigs. These metal balls are painted to look like an insect's head. Some jigs have strings of feathers or animal hair attached to them. Anglers place jigs near the bottom of a body of water. Some anglers add bait to jigs.

Freshwater Methods

Anglers in boats can use various methods to catch fish. They may allow the boat to drift with the wind and currents. They may troll, which involves using a small motor to move the boat slowly through the water. They cast the bait or lure behind the boat. They then set the drag to keep the line tight. The movement of the bait or lure attracts fish.

From shore, anglers often cast out and reel in lures. Other shore anglers use bait. They cast and wait for fish to take the bait. In streams and rivers, anglers cast upstream and let the current carry the bait or lure downstream.

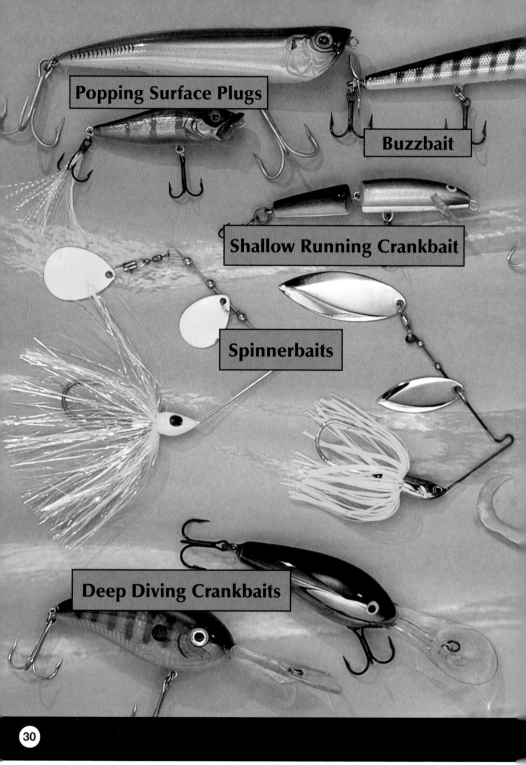

Popping Surface Plugs

Buzzbait

Shallow Running Crankbait

Spinnerbaits

Deep Diving Crankbaits

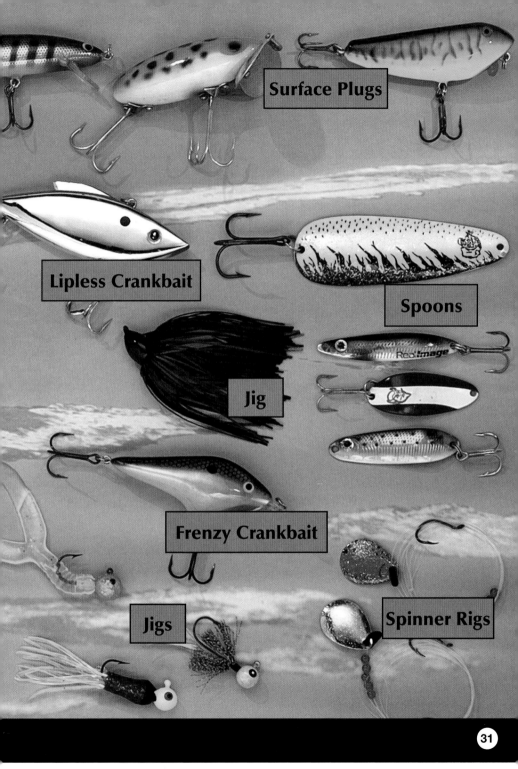

Surface Plugs

Lipless Crankbait

Spoons

Jig

Frenzy Crankbait

Jigs

Spinner Rigs

Chapter 4

CONSERVATION

Learn about catch and release, water pollution, and fishing licenses.

Responsible anglers protect fish and their habitats. Anglers should dispose of garbage and used fishing line properly. Fish and other wildlife may become entangled in fishing line or other items. Responsible anglers do not trample on plants or disturb wildlife.

Conservation Problems

Anglers who are not responsible can harm the environment. People sometimes take too many fish out of freshwater sources. This can change the balance of fish populations. For example, people may take too many large fish such as pike and muskellunge out of a lake. This causes the water source to become overpopulated with panfish, which are the prey of muskellunge and pike.

Government agencies sometimes stock fish in water sources that have decreasing fish populations.

Pollution can damage freshwater sources. Farmers use fertilizer to make their crops grow. They use herbicides to kill weeds. These chemicals can enter water sources. Sewage and industrial wastes can also enter water supplies.

Polluted water causes many fish to die. Some fish can live in polluted waters. But poisons may build up in their bodies. This makes the fish dangerous to eat.

Freshwater Improvements

Laws help prevent further pollution of the nation's water sources. In 1972, the U.S. government passed the Clean Water Act. This law set guidelines for how industries should dispose of their wastes.

The U.S. Fish and Wildlife Service conserves, restores, and manages fish habitats in the United States. It also establishes wildlife refuges to protect fish, birds, and other animals. Hunting and fishing is limited or illegal in these areas.

The National Fish Hatchery System is part of the U.S. Fish and Wildlife Service. Members of this system raise fish in hatcheries. They then release the fish into water sources with low fish populations.

Many people form groups to improve fish habitats and increase fish populations. For example, Trout Unlimited and the Nature Conservancy replace plants and gravel beds that help fish spawn. Fish lay eggs when they spawn.

hatchery—a place where people allow fish eggs to hatch

Anglers should only fish in areas where it is safe and allowed by law.

Licenses and Regulations

North American anglers need to follow all state or province regulations. These regulations vary in the United States and Canada. Anglers of a certain age or older must buy fishing licenses. This age ranges from about 12 to 16. Anglers buy separate licenses when they fish away from their home state or province.

Limits regulate the number of fish a person can catch in one day. These limits vary according to the species and time of year.

People may catch most fish year-round. But some states and provinces have fishing seasons for certain fish species. For example, some provinces do not allow bass fishing until June. This regulation allows young fish to grow large enough to protect themselves. Some states do not allow people to fish in certain streams and rivers during spawning times.

Chapter 5

SAFETY

Learn about weather safety, handling fish, and safe boating.

All anglers should follow safety guidelines. They should know the weather forecast and be prepared for severe weather. They should know basic first aid skills and be prepared for accidents.

Storms

Anglers pay attention to the weather forecast before they go fishing. They look for signs of approaching storms as they fish. Anglers may notice large, gray clouds or feel a sudden rush of cold air before storms. Many anglers have a radio to listen to weather forecasts.

Anglers in boats head for shore if a storm occurs. Anglers on shore stay away from tall trees, peaks, and other high objects. Lightning is more likely to strike these areas.

Safe anglers are aware of their surroundings when they cast.

Other Safety Guidelines

Anglers must handle fish carefully. They keep their hands away from the fish's mouth and spine. Some fish have sharp fins on their backs. Other fish such as perch and walleye have sharp gill covers. Fish breathe through gills. These openings are along the sides of a fish.

Anglers follow other safety guidelines. They stay away from litter that could cut or entangle them. Anglers in boats watch wave conditions. They learn where sandbars and other underwater objects are located.

Anglers need to be careful when they fish near streams and rivers. Rocks on riverbanks may be slippery. Rivers and streams might have powerful currents or underwater drop-offs. Water suddenly becomes deep at these places. Anglers should avoid entering a stream or river.

Safe anglers are prepared for unexpected situations, and they are aware of their surroundings.

Anglers should know how to use the items in their first aid kits. These items usually include gloves, medicine tape, tweezers, scissors, and bandages. They also have gauze to cover wounds. Most kits have ointment to protect wounds from germs.

Rainbow Trout

Description: Rainbow trout have silver skin covered with small black spots. A pink-orange band usually runs lengthwise along their sides. Their backs are blue-green to olive. Rainbow trout usually weigh about 2 pounds (.9 kilogram).

Habitat: cool, quickly flowing rivers and streams; some cool lakes

Food: fish eggs, minnows, small fish

Bait and lures: nightcrawlers, minnows, salmon eggs, marshmallows, spinners, spoons, small minnow imitations, small plugs

Walleye

Description: Walleye vary in color. They may be various shades of silver, yellow, yellow-red, or yellow-blue. They have small spots above their white undersides. Walleye have large eyes. They usually weigh about 1 to 40 pounds (.45 to 18 kilograms).

Habitat: open areas in large lakes; cold, deep water near drop-offs and weeds in lakes

Food: minnows, small fish

Bait and lures: nightcrawlers, minnows, spinners, deep diving spoons, plugs

Bluegill

Description: Bluegill are bronze with dark bars on their sides. They have a large black spot on the edge of their gill covers. Bluegill usually weigh about 1/2 pound to 1 pound (.2 to .5 kilogram).

Habitat: ponds, lakes, slow-moving rivers and streams with sandy bottoms; weedy areas, near roots and structures, shallow water close to shore

Food: insects, plants, fish eggs, small fish, snails, worms

Bait and lures: crickets, worms, caterpillars, grubs, grasshoppers, small spinners

Largemouth Bass

Description: Largemouth bass vary in color from green to dark gray. Most of these fish have a green back. Largemouth bass have a mouth that extends beyond the eye. They usually weigh about 2 to 6 pounds (.9 to 2.7 kilograms).

Habitat: weedy, warm water in lakes and streams

Food: insects, minnows, frogs, small fish, snakes, turtles, ducklings, crawfish

Bait and lures: nightcrawlers, plugs, spinners, plastic worms, jigs

GLOSSARY

barb (BARB)—a sharp piece of metal that extends from behind a fishhook's point

drag (DRAG)—the device that places pressure on the line; anglers often adjust the reel's drag after they hook a fish.

edge (EJ)—a visible line where water changes or plants grow

habitat (HAB-uh-tat)—the natural place and conditions in which animals live

hatchery (HACH-er-ee)—a place where people allow fish eggs to hatch

plankton (PLANGK-tuhn)—tiny animals and plants that usually drift or float in oceans or lakes

spawning time (SPAH-ning TIME)—when fish lay eggs

species (SPEE-sheez)—a group of animals with similar features

READ MORE

Klobuchar, Lisa. *Fishing.* Get Going! Hobbies. Chicago: Heinemann Library, 2006.

Slade, Suzanne. *Let's go Fishing.* Adventures Outdoors. New York: Rosen, 2007.

INTERNET SITES

FactHound offers a safe, fun way to find Internet sites related to this book. All of the sites on FactHound have been researched by our staff.

Here's how:

1. Visit *www.facthound.com*

2. Choose your grade level.

3. Type in this book ID **142960820X** for age-appropriate sites. You may also browse subjects by clicking on letters, or by clicking pictures and words.

4. Click on the **Fetch It** button.

FactHound will fetch the best sites for you!

INDEX